THE ROLE OF THE INDIVIDUAL
IN HISTORY

THE
ROLE OF THE INDIVIDUAL
IN HISTORY

BY

G. V. PLEKHANOV

University Press of the Pacific
Honolulu, Hawaii

The Role of the Individual in History

by
Georgi Valentinovich Plekhanov

ISBN: 1-4102-0948-2

University Press of the Pacific
Honolulu, Hawaii
http://www.universitypressofthepacific.com

PREFACE

PLEKHANOV'S essay, "The Role of the Individual in History," was first published in 1898 in *Nauchnoye Obozrenie* under the *nom de plume* of A. Kirsanov. Subsequently it was included in the selection of Plekhanov's works entitled *Twenty Years*. In the *Complete Works* (Russian Edition) it is to be found in Vol. VIII, published in 1925.

This essay occupies a very prominent place among those of Plekhanov's works in which he substantiates and defends Marxism and advocates the Marxian theory of social development.

The opponents of Marxism long ago argued that Marxism repudiated the role and significance of the individual in social development and that it converted historical progress itself into something fatalistic, nameless and impersonal. This false argument was put forward with particular zeal in the nineties of the last century by the Russian Narodniks, the bitterest enemies of Marxism.

Plekhanov's essay played a very important part in exposing this slanderous argument against Marxism and in explaining the real views of Marxism as to the role of the individual in history.

This essay may be regarded as one of the best in Marxist literature. Excellently written, picturesque in style and sparkling with wit, it holds the reader even to-day and helps him properly to understand the problem of the role of the individual in social development.

Besides being a brilliant exposition of the views of Marxism on the role of the individual in history, this essay delivered a crushing blow to one of the fundamental principles of Narodnik theory—namely, the theory of "heroes" and the "mob," according to which human history develops, not as a process expressing definite laws, but only in accidental ways, in accordance with the prescriptions and fantasies of "critically thinking individuals"; it is made only by "heroes," while the masses of the people remain an "inert force," a "mob"; he (the "hero") "cannot help looking down upon it, cannot help realising that everything depends upon him, the hero, whereas the mob is a mass, totally lacking the creative element and only to be compared to an enormous number of noughts, which acquire beneficent significance only when a kind, 'critically thinking' unit condescendingly takes its place at their head" (Plekhanov, *The Development of the Monistic Conception of History*, Complete Works, Vol. VII, p. 156, Russian edition). Plekhanov utterly shattered these views and simultaneously shattered the political conclusions which the Narodniks (and subsequently the Socialist-Revolutionaries) drew from this "theory"—namely, that the masses must abandon the revolutionary struggle, that individual terrorism must be adopted, which excludes the organisation of a mass revolutionary party.

In this essay Plekhanov also shattered the arguments of the direct apologists of capitalism, who, because the character of social development is governed by laws, tried to find "theoretical" grounds for the argument that the workers must abandon the struggle against capitalism, thus striving to eliminate the principal driving force in historical progress, namely, the revolutionary class and the leaders of the revolutionary class.

The open champions and apologists of capitalism also tried to proclaim as the true spirit of Marxism the stupid thesis which the Narodniks, in deliberately perverting Marxism, attributed to it, *viz.,* as social development is a process conforming to laws, "the individual can do nothing." Plekhanov also frustrated this attempt. Human history as a process expresses laws, but does not proceed independently of man; history is made by men who set the problems of progress and solve them in conformity with the historical conditions of the epoch. Hence, the activity of men cannot but be of enormous significance in history, and Plekhanov clearly revealed and proved the exceptional role which prominent individuals can play in history. He says in this essay that a great man is great because "he possesses qualities which make him most capable of serving the great social needs of his time, needs which arise as a result of general and particular causes. Carlyle, in his well-known book on heroes and hero-worship, calls great men *beginners.* This is a very apt description. A great man is precisely a beginner because he sees *further* than others and desires things *more strongly* than others."

The strength of an outstanding individual lies in his contact with a class, with the masses, with the people; his strength lies in his ability to organise the masses, in his ability to foresee the course of historical progress. Without this ability, the role of the individual is reduced to nought. Emphasising the great strength of the masses

7

as the genuine makers of history, Stalin says: "Only the people are immortal. Everything else is transient. That is why we must be able to value the confidence of the people."

Notwithstanding the fact that subsequently Plekhanov, isolating himself from the masses, became politically lame, as it were, the present essay retains its enormous significance to this day. It can help our young people to understand properly the Marxian tenets on the role of the individual in history and to combat the survivals of Narodnik and Socialist Revolutionary views on this question.

Lenin wrote that "his [Plekhanov's] personal services in the past were enormous. During the twenty years 1883-1903 he produced a large number of excellent works, particularly in opposition to the opportunists, Machists and Narodniks" (*Collected Works*, Vol. XVII, pp. 415-16, Russian edition). Lenin urged young Communists to study Plekhanov's philosophical works, and insisted on their republication and inclusion in a "series of obligatory text books on Communism" (*Collected Works*, Vol. XXVI, p. 135, Russian edition).

I

IN the second half of the 'seventies the late Kablitz wrote an article entitled, "The Mind and the Senses as Factors of Progress," in which, referring to Spencer, he argued that the senses played the principal role in human progress, and that the mind played only a secondary role, and quite a subordinate one at that. A certain "esteemed sociologist" replied to Kablitz, expressing amusement and surprise at a theory which placed the mind "on the footboard." The "esteemed sociologist" was right, of course, in defending the mind. He would have been much more right, however, had he, without going into the details of the question that Kablitz had raised, proved that his very method of presenting it was impossible and impermissible. Indeed, the "factors" theory is unsound in itself, for it arbitrarily picks out different sides of social life, hypostasises them, converts them into forces of a special kind, which, from different sides, and with unequal success, draw the social man along the path of progress. But this theory is still less sound in the form presented by Kablitz, who converted into special sociological hypostases, not the various sides of the activities of the *social man*, but the different spheres of the *individual mind*. This is a veritable Herculean pillar of abstraction; beyond this one cannot go, for beyond it lies the comic kingdom of utter and obvious absurdity. It is to this that the "esteemed sociologist" should have drawn the attention of Kablitz and his readers. Perhaps,

9

after revealing the depths of abstraction into which the effort to find the predominating "factor" in history had led Kablitz, the "esteemed sociologist" might, by chance, have made some contribution to the critique of this factors theory. This would have been very useful for all of us at that time. But he proved unequal to his mission. He himself subscribed to that theory, differing from Kablitz only in his leanings towards *eclecticism*, and consequently, all the "factors" seemed to him to be equally important. Subsequently, the eclectic nature of his mind found particularly striking expression in his attacks on dialectical materialism, which he regarded as a doctrine which sacrifices all other factors to the economic "factor" and reduces the role of the individual in history to nothing. It never occurred to the "esteemed sociologist" that the "factors" point of view is alien to dialectical materialism, and that only one who is utterly incapable of thinking logically can see in it any justification of so-called *quietism*. Incidentally, it must be observed that the slip made by our "esteemed sociologist" is not unique; very many others have made it, are making it and, probably, will go on making it.

Materialists began to be accused of betraying leanings towards quietism even before they had worked out their dialectical conception of Nature and of history. Without making an excursion into the "depth of time," we will recall the controversy between the celebrated English scientist, Priestley, and Price. Analysing Priestley's theories, Price argued that materialism was incompatible with the concept free will, and that it precluded all independent activity on the part of the individual. In reply Priestley referred to everyday experience. He would not speak of himself, he said, though by no means the most apathetic of creatures, but where would one find more mental vigour, more activity, more force and persistence in the pursuit of extremely important aims, than among those who subscribe to the doctrine of necessity? Priestley had in view the religious, democratic sect then known as Christian Necessarians.[1] We do not know whether this sect was as active as Priestley, who belonged to it, thought it was. But that is not important. There cannot be the slightest doubt that the materialist conception of the human will is quite compatible with the most vigorous practical activity. Lanson observes that "all the doctrines which called for the utmost exertion of human will asserted, in principle, that the will was impotent; they rejected free will and subjected the world to fatalism."[2] Lanson was wrong in thinking that every repudiation of what is called free will leads to fatalism; but this did not prevent him from noting an extremely interesting historical fact. Indeed, history shows that even fatalism was not always a hindrance to energetic, practical action; on the contrary, in certain epochs it was a *psychologically necessary basis for such action*. In proof of this, we will point to the Puritans, who in energy excelled all the other parties in England in the seventeenth century; and to the followers of Mohammed, who in a

[1] A Frenchman of the seventeenth century would have been surprised at this combination of materialism and religious dogma. In England, however, nobody thought it strange. Priestley himself was very religious. Different countries, different customs.

[2] Cf. his *Histoire de la littérature française*, Vol. I.

short space of time subjugated an enormous part of the globe, stretching from India to Spain. Those who think that the conviction that a certain series of events is inevitable is sufficient to cause all psychological possibility of helping on, or counteracting, these events to disappear, are very much mistaken.[1]

Here, everything depends upon whether my activities constitute an inevitable link in the chain of inevitable events. If they do, then I waver less and the more resolute are my actions. There is nothing surprising in this: when we say that a certain individual regards his activities as an inevitable link in the chain of inevitable events, we mean, among other things, that for this individual, lack of free will is tantamount to *incapability of inaction*, and that this lack of free will is reflected in his mind as the *impossibility of acting differently from the way he is acting*. This is precisely the psychological mood that can be expressed in the celebrated words of Luther: "*Here I stand, I can do no other*," and thanks to which men

---

[1] It is well known that, according to the doctrines of Calvin, all men's actions are predetermined by God: "*By predestination we mean the eternal decree of God, by which he within himself has ordained what it behoves shall happen to each man*" (*Institutio*, Book III, Ch. 5). According to the same doctrine, God chooses certain of his servants to liberate unjustly oppressed peoples. Such a one was Moses, who liberated the people of Israel. Everything goes to show that Cromwell also regarded himself as such an instrument of God; he always called his actions the fruits of the will of God, and probably, he was quite sincerely convinced that they were so. *For him*, all these actions were *coloured by necessity beforehand*. This did not prevent him from striving for victory after victory; it even gave this striving indomitable power.

display the most indomitable energy, perform the most astonishing feats. Hamlet never knew this mood; that is why he was only capable of moaning and reflecting. And that is why Hamlet would never have accepted a philosophy, according to which freedom is merely necessity transformed into mind. Fichte rightly said: "*As the man is, so is his philosophy.*"

II

SOME people here have taken seriously Stammler's remarks about the allegedly insoluble contradiction that is said to be characteristic of a certain West European social-political theory.[1] We have in mind the well-known example of the eclipse of the moon. As a matter of fact, this is a supremely absurd example. The combination of conditions that are necessary to cause an eclipse of the moon does not, and cannot under any circumstances, include human action; and, for this reason alone, projects to assist the eclipse of the moon can arise only in a lunatic asylum. But even if human action did serve as one of these conditions, none of those who keenly desired to see an eclipse of the moon would, if they were convinced that it would certainly take place *without their aid*, join the eclipse of the moon party. In this case, "quietism" would merely be abstention from *unnecessary, i.e. useless, action* and would have no affinity with real quietism. In

[1] I.e. Marxism.—TRANS.

13

order that the example of the eclipse of the moon may cease to be nonsensical in the case of the above-mentioned party that we are examining, it must be entirely changed. It would have to be imagined that the moon is gifted with a mind, and that her position in celestial space, which causes her eclipse, appears to her to be the fruit of the self-determination of her own will; that it not only gives her enormous pleasure, but is absolutely necessary for her peace of mind; and that this is why she always passionately strives to occupy this position.[1] After imagining all this, the question would have to be asked: What would the moon feel if she discovered, at last, that it is not her will, and not her "ideals," that determine her movement in celestial space, but, on the contrary, that her movement determines her will and her "ideals"? According to Stammler, such a discovery would certainly make her incapable of moving, unless she succeeded in extricating herself from her predicament by some logical contradiction. But such an assumption is totally groundless. This discovery might serve as a *formal* reason for the moon's bad temper, for feeling out of harmony with herself, for the contradiction between her "ideals" and mechanical reality. But since we are assuming that the "moon's psychological state" *in general* is, in the last analysis, determined by her movement, then the cause of her disturbed peace of mind must be sought for in her movement. If this subject were examined carefully

[1] "It is as if the compass needle took pleasure in turning towards the north, believing that its movement was independent of any other cause, and unaware of the imperceptible movements of magnetic matter." Leibnitz, *Théodicée*, Lausanne, 1760, p. 598.

14

it would have transpired, perhaps, that when the moon was at her apogee she grieved over the fact that her will was not free; and when she was at her perigee, this very circumstance served as a new, formal cause of her happiness and good spirits. Perhaps, the opposite would have happened: perhaps it would have transpired that she found the means of reconciling free will with necessity, not at her perigee, but at her apogee. Be that as it may, such a reconciliation is undoubtedly possible; being conscious of necessity is quite compatible with the most energetic, practical action. At all events, this has been the case in history so far. Men who have repudiated free will have often excelled all their contemporaries in strength of will, and asserted their will to the utmost. Numerous examples of this can be quoted. They are universally known. They can be forgotten, as Stammler evidently does, only if one deliberately refuses to see historical reality as it actually is. This attitude is strongly marked, among our subjectivists for example, and among some German philistines. Philistines and subjectivists, however, are not men, but mere *phantoms*, as Belinsky would have said.

Let us, however, examine more closely the case when a man's own—past, present or future—actions seem to him to be entirely coloured by necessity. We know already that such a man, regarding himself as a messenger of God, like Mohammed, as one chosen by ineluctable destiny, like Napoleon, or as the expression of the irresistible force of historical progress, like some of the public men in the nineteenth century, displays almost elemental strength of will, and sweeps from his path like

15

a house of cards all the obstacles set up by the small-town Hamlets and Hamletkins.[1] But this case interests us now from another angle—namely, as follows: When the consciousness of my lack of free will presents itself to me only in the form of the complete subjective and objective impossibility of acting differently from the way I am acting, and when, at the same time, my actions are to me the most desirable of all other possible actions, then, in my mind, necessity becomes identified with freedom and freedom with necessity; and then, I am unfree only in the sense *that I cannot disturb this identity between freedom and necessity, I cannot oppose one to the other, I cannot feel the restraint of necessity. But such a lack of freedom* is at the same time its *fullest manifestation.*

Zimmel says that freedom is always freedom from something, and, where freedom is not conceived as the opposite of restraint, it is meaningless. That is so, of course. But this slight, elementary truth cannot serve as a ground for refuting the thesis, which constitutes one

[1] We will quote another example, which vividly illustrates how strongly people of this category feel. In a letter to her teacher, Calvin, Renée, Duchess of Ferrara (of the house of Louis XII) wrote as follows: "No, I have not forgotten what you wrote to me: that David bore mortal hatred towards the enemies of God. And I will never act differently, for if I knew that the King, my father, the Queen, my mother, the late lord, my husband (*feu monsieur mon mari*) and all my children had been cast out by God, I would hate them with a mortal hatred and would wish them in Hell," etc. What terrible, all-destroying energy the people who felt like this could display! And yet these people denied that there was such a thing as free will.

of the most brilliant discoveries ever made by philosophic thought, that freedom means being conscious of necessity. Zimmel's definition is too narrow: it applies only to freedom from external restraint. As long as we are discussing only such restraints it would be extremely ridiculous to identify freedom with necessity: a pickpocket is not free to steal your pocket-handkerchief while you are preventing him from doing so and until he has overcome your resistance in one way or another. In addition to this elementary and superficial conception of freedom, however, there is another, incomparably more profound. For those who are incapable of thinking philosophically this concept does not exist at all; and those who are capable of thinking philosophically grasp it only when they have cast off dualism and realise that, contrary to the assumption of the dualists, there is no gulf between the subject and the object.

The Russian subjectivist opposes his utopian ideals to our capitalist reality and goes no further. The subjectivists have stuck in the bog of *dualism*. The ideals of the so-called Russian "disciples"[1] resemble capitalist reality far less than the ideals of the subjectivists. Notwithstanding this, however, the "disciples" have found a bridge which unites ideals with reality. The "disciples" have elevated themselves to *monism*. In their opinion, capitalism, in the course of its development, will lead to its own negation and to the realisation of their, the Russian "disciples'"—and not only the Russian—ideals. This is historical *necessity. The "disciple" serves as an instrument*

[1] I.e. the Marxists.—TRANS.

of this necessity and cannot help doing so, owing to his social status and to his mentality and temperament, which were created by his status. This, too, is an *aspect of necessity.* Since his social status has imbued him with this character and no other, he not only serves as an instrument of necessity and cannot help doing so, but he *passionately desires, and cannot help desiring,* to do so. This is *an aspect of freedom,* and, moreover, of freedom that has grown out of necessity, i.e. to put it more correctly, it is freedom that is identical with necessity—it is necessity transformed into freedom.[1] *This* freedom is also freedom from a certain amount of restraint; it is also the antithesis of a certain amount of restriction. Profound definitions do not refute superficial ones, but, supplementing them, include them in themselves. But what sort of restraint, what sort of restriction, is in question in this case? This is clear: the moral restraint which curbs the energy of those who have not cast off dualism; the restriction suffered by those who are unable to bridge the gulf between ideals and reality. Until the individual has won *this* freedom by heroic effort in philosophical thinking he does not fully belong to himself, and his mental tortures are the shameful tribute he pays to external necessity that stands opposed to him. But as soon as this individual throws off the yoke of this painful and shameful restriction he is born for a new, full and hitherto never experienced life; and his *free* actions become the *conscious and free* expression of *necessity.* Then he will become a

[1] "Necessity becomes freedom, not by disappearing, but only by the external expression of their inner identity." Hegel, *Wissenschaft der Logik,* 1816.

great social force; and then nothing can, and nothing will, prevent him from

> Bursting on cunning falsehood
> Like a storm of wrath divine . . .

III

AGAIN, being conscious of the absolute inevitability of a given phenomenon can only increase the energy of a man who sympathises with it and who regards himself as one of the forces which called it into being. If such a man, conscious of the inevitability of this phenomenon, folded his arms and did nothing, he would show that he was ignorant of arithmetic. Indeed, let us suppose that phenomenon A must necessarily take place under a given sum of circumstances. You have proved to me that a part of this sum of circumstances already exists and that the other part will exist in a given time, T. Being convinced of this, I, the man who sympathises with phenomenon A, exclaim: "Good!" and then go to sleep until the happy day when the event you have foretold takes place. What will be the result? The following. In your calculations, the sum of circumstances necessary to bring about phenomenon A, included *my activities*, equal, let us say to a. As, however, I am immersed in deep slumber, the sum of circumstances favourable for the given phenomenon at time T will be, not S, but $S - a$, which changes the situation. Perhaps my place will be taken by another man, who was also on the point of inaction, but was saved by the sight of my apathy, which to him appeared to be pernicious. In that case, force a will be replaced by force b, and if a equals b $(a=b)$, the sum of circumstances favourable for A will remain equal to S, and phenomenon A will take place, after all, at time T.

But if my force cannot be regarded as being equal to zero, if I am a skilful and capable worker, and nobody has replaced me, then we will not have the full sum S, and phenomenon A will take place later than we assumed, or not as fully as we expected, or it may not take place at all. This is as clear as daylight; and if I do not understand it, if I think that S remains S even after I am replaced, it is only because I am unable to count. But am I the only one who is unable to count? You, who prophesied that the sum S would certainly be available at time T, did not foresee that I would go to sleep immediately after my conversation with you; you were convinced that I would remain a good worker to the end; the force was less reliable than you thought. Hence, you, too, counted badly. But let us suppose that you had made no mistake, that you had made allowance for everything. In that case, your calculations will assume the following form: you say that at time T the sum S will be available. This sum of circumstances will include my replacement as a *negative magnitude*; and it will also include, as a *positive magnitude*, the stimulating effect on strong-minded men of the conviction that their strivings and ideals are the subjective expression of objective necessity. In that case, the sum S will indeed be available at the time you

20

appointed, and phenomenon A will take place. I think this is clear. But if this is clear, why was I confused by the idea that phenomenon A was inevitable? Why did it seem to me that it condemned me to inaction? Why, in discussing it, did I forget the simplest rules of arithmetic? Probably because, owing to the circumstances of my upbringing, I already had a very strong leaning towards inaction and my conversation with you served as the drop which filled the cup of this laudable inclination to overflowing. That is all. *Only in this sense—as the cause that revealed my moral flabbiness and uselessness—did the consciousness of necessity figure here.* It cannot possibly be regarded as the *cause* of this flabbiness: the causes of it are the circumstances of my upbringing. And so . . . and so—arithmetic is a very respectable and useful science, the rules of which should not be forgotten even by—I would say, particularly by—philosophers.

But what effect will the consciousness of the necessity of a given phenomenon have upon a strong man who does *not sympathise* with it and *resists* its taking place? Here the situation is somewhat different. It is very possible that it will cause the vigour of his resistance to *relax*. But when do the opponents of a given phenomenon become convinced that it is inevitable? When the circumstances favourable to it are very numerous and very strong. The fact that its opponents realise that the phenomenon is inevitable, and the relaxation of their energy, are merely manifestations of the force of circumstances favourable to it. These manifestations, in their turn, are a part of the favourable circumstances.

But the vigour of resistance will not be relaxed among

all the opponents; among some of them the conscious-ness that the phenomenon is inevitable will cause it to grow and become transformed into the vigour of *despair*. History in general, and the history of Russia in particular, provides not a few instructive examples of this sort of vigour. We hope the reader will be able to recall these without our assistance.

Here we are interrupted by Mr. Kareyev, who, while, of course, disagreeing with our views on freedom and necessity, and, moreover, disapproving of our partiality for the "extremes" to which strong men go, nevertheless, is pleased to meet in the pages of our journal the idea that the individual may be a great social force. The worthy Professor joyfully exclaims: "I have always said that!" And this is true. Mr. Kareyev, and all the subjectivists, have always ascribed a very important role to the individual in history. And there was a time when they enjoyed considerable sympathy among advanced young people who were imbued with noble strivings to work for the common weal and were, therefore, naturally inclined to attach great importance to individual initia-tive. In essence, however, the subjectivists have never been able to solve, or even to present properly, the problem of the role of the individual in history. As against the influence of the *laws* of social-historical progress, they advanced the "activities of critically thinking individuals," and thus created, as it were, a new species of the factors theory; critically thinking indivi-duals were *one factor* of this progress; its own laws were the *other* factor. This resulted in an extreme incongruity, which one could put up with as long as the attention of the active "individuals" was concentrated on the practical problems of the day and they had no time to devote to philosophical problems. But the calm which ensued in the 'eighties gave those who were capable of thinking enforced leisure for philosophical reflection, and since then, the subjectivist doctrine has been bursting at all its seams, and even falling to pieces, like the celebrated overcoat of Acacii Acacievich. No amount of patching was of any use, and one after another thinking people began to reject subjectivism as an obviously and utterly unsound doctrine. As always happens in such cases, however, the reaction against this doctrine caused some of its opponents to go to the opposite extreme. While some subjectivists, striving to ascribe the widest possible role to the "individual" in history, refused to recognise the historical progress of mankind as a process expressing laws, some of their later opponents, striving to bring out more sharply the coherent character of this progress, were evidently prepared to forget that *men make history, and therefore, the activities of individuals cannot help being important in history.* They have declared the individual to be a *quantité négligeable.* In theory, this extreme is as impermissible as the one reached by the more ardent subjectivists. It is as unsound to sacrifice the *thesis to the antithesis* as to forget the antithesis for the sake of the *thesis.* The correct point of view will be found only when we succeed in uniting the points of truth contained in them into a *synthesis.*[1]

[1] In our striving for a synthesis, we were forestalled by the same Mr. Kareyev. Unfortunately, however, he went no farther than to admit the truism that man consists of a soul and a body.

23

IV

THIS problem has been interesting us for a long time, and we have long wanted to invite our readers to join us in tackling it. We were restrained, however, by certain fears: we thought that perhaps our readers had already solved it for themselves and that our proposal would be belated. These fears have now been dispelled. The German historians have dispelled them for us. We are quite serious in saying this. The fact of the matter is that lately a rather heated controversy has been going on among the German historians over great men in history. Some have been inclined to regard the political activities of these men as the main and almost the only spring of historical development, while others have been asserting that such a view is one-sided and that the science of history must have in view, not only the activities of great men, and not only political history, but historical life as a whole (*das Ganze des geschichtilichen Lebens*). One of the representatives of the latter trend is Karl Lamprecht, author of *The History of the German People*, translated into Russian by P. Nikolayev. Lamprecht's opponents accused him of being a "*collectivist*" and a materialist; he was even placed on a par with—*horribile dictu*—the "Social-Democratic atheists," as he expressed it in winding up the debate. When we became acquainted with his views we found that the accusations hurled against this poor savant were utterly groundless. At the same time we were convinced that the present-day German historians were incapable of solving the problem of the role of the individual in history. We then decided that we had a right to assume that the problem was still unsolved even for a number of Russian readers, and that something could still be said about it that would not be altogether lacking in theoretical and practical interest.

Lamprecht gathered a whole collection (*eine artige Sammlung*, as he expresses it) of the views of prominent statesmen on their own activities in the historical milieu in which they pursued them; in his polemics, however, he confined himself for the time being to references to some of the speeches and opinions of *Bismarck*. He quoted the following words, uttered by the Iron Chancellor in the North German Reichstag on April 16, 1869:

"Gentlemen, we can neither ignore the history of the past nor create the future. I would like to warn you against the mistake that causes people to advance the hands of their clocks, thinking that thereby they are hastening the passage of time. My influence on the events I took advantage of is usually exaggerated; but it would never occur to anyone to demand that *I should make history*. I could not do that even in conjunction with you, although together, we could resist the whole world. We cannot make history: we must wait while it is being made. We will not make fruit ripen more quickly by subjecting it to the heat of a lamp; and if we pluck the fruit before it is ripe we will only prevent its growth and spoil it."

Referring to the evidence of Joly, Lamprecht also quotes the opinions which Bismarck expressed more than once during the Franco-Prussian war. Again, the idea that runs through these opinions is that "we cannot make great historical events, but must adapt ourselves to the natural course of things and limit ourselves to securing what is already ripe." Lamprecht regards this as the profound and whole truth. In his opinion, a modern historian cannot think otherwise, provided he is able to peer into the depths of events and not restrict his field of vision to too short an interval of time. Could Bismarck have caused Germany to revert to natural economy? He would have been unable to do this even when he was at the height of his power. General historical circumstances are stronger than the strongest individuals. For a great man, the general character of his epoch is *"empirically given necessity."*

This is how Lamprecht reasons, calling his view a *universal* one. It is not difficult to see the weak side of this "universal" view. The above-quoted opinions of Bismarck are very interesting as a psychological document. One may not sympathise with the activities of the late German Chancellor, but one cannot say that they were insignificant, that Bismarck was distinguished for "quietism." It was about him that Lassalle said: "The servants of reaction are no orators; but God grant that progress has servants like them." And yet this man, who at times displayed truly iron energy, considered himself absolutely impotent in face of the natural course of things, evidently regarding himself as a simple instrument of historical development: this proves once again that one can see phenomena in the light of necessity and at the same time be a very energetic statesman. But it is only in this respect that Bismarck's opinions are interesting;

26

they cannot be regarded as a solution of the problem of the role of the individual in history. According to Bismarck, events occur of themselves, and we can secure what they prepare for us. But every act of "securing" is also an historical event: what is the difference between such events and those that occur of themselves? Actually, nearly every historical event is simultaneously an act of "securing" by somebody of the already ripened fruit of preceding development and a link in the chain of events which are preparing the fruits of the future. How can acts of "securing" be opposed to the natural course of things? Evidently, Bismarck wanted to say that individuals and groups of individuals operating in history never were and never will be all-powerful. This, of course, is beyond all doubt. Nevertheless, we would like to know what their power, far from omnipotence, of course, depends on; under what circumstances it grows and under what circumstances it diminishes. Neither Bismarck nor the learned advocate of the "universal" conception of history who quotes him, answers these questions.

It is true that Lamprecht gives us more reasonable quotations.[1] For example, he quotes the following words of Monod, one of the most prominent representatives of contemporary historical science in France:

"Historians are too much in the habit of paying attention only to the brilliant, clamorous and ephemeral

[1] Leaving aside Lamprecht's other philosophical and historical essays, we refer to his essay, "Der Ausgang des geschichtswissenschaftlichen Kampfes," *Die Zukunft*, 1897, No. 41.

manifestations of human activity, to great events and great men, instead of depicting the great and slow changes of economic conditions and social institutions, which constitute the really interesting and intransient part of human development—the part which, to a certain extent, may be reduced to laws and subjected, to a certain extent, to exact analysis. Indeed, important events and individuals are important precisely as signs and symbols of different moments of the aforesaid development. But most of the events that are called historical have the same relation to real history as the waves which rise up from the surface of the sea, gleam in the light for a moment and break on the sandy shore, leaving no trace behind them, have to the deep and constant motion of the tides."

Lamprecht declares that he is prepared to put• his signature to every one of these words. It is well known that German savants are reluctant to agree with French savants and the French are reluctant to agree with the German. That is why the Belgian historian Pirenne was particularly pleased to emphasise in *Revue Historique* the fact that Monod's conception of history coincides with that of Lamprecht. "This harmony is extremely significant," he observed. "Evidently, it shows that the future belongs to the new conception of history."

V

WE do not share Pirenne's pleasant expectations. The future cannot belong to vague and indefinite views, and such, precisely, are the views of Monod and particularly of Lamprecht. Of course, one cannot but welcome a trend that declares that the most important task of the science of history is to study social institutions and economic conditions. This science will make great progress when such a trend becomes definitely consolidated. In the first place, however, Pirenne is wrong in thinking that this is a new trend. It arose in the science of history as far back as the twenties of the nineteenth century: Guizot, Mignet, Augustin Thierry and, subsequently, Tocqueville and others, were its brilliant and consistent representatives. The views of Monod and Lamprecht are but a faint copy of an old but excellent original. Secondly, profound as the views of Guizot, Mignet and the other French historians may have been for their time, much in them has remained unelucidated. They do not provide a full and definite solution of the problem of the role of the individual in history. And the science of history must provide this solution if its representatives are destined to rid themselves of their one-sided conception of their subject. The future belongs to the school that finds the best solution of this problem, among others.

The views of Guizot, Mignet and the other historians who belonged to this trend were a reaction against the views on history that prevailed in the eighteenth century and constituted their *antithesis*. In the eighteenth century the students of the philosophy of history reduced everything to the *conscious activities of individuals*. True, there were exceptions to the rule even at that time: the philosophical-historical field of vision of Vice, Montesquieu and Herder, for example, was much wider. But we are not speaking of exceptions; the great majority of the thinkers of the eighteenth century regarded history exactly in the way we have described. In this connection it is very interesting to peruse once again the historical works of Mably, for example. According to Mably, Minos created the whole of the social and political life and ethics of the Cretes, while Lycurgus performed the same service for Sparta. If the Spartans "spurned" material wealth, it was due entirely to Lycurgus, who "descended, so to speak, into the depths of the hearts of his fellow-citizens and there crushed the germ of love for wealth" (*descendit pour ainsi dire jusque dans le fond du cœur des citoyens,* etc.).[1] And if, subsequently, the Spartans strayed from the path the wise Lycurgus had pointed out to them, the blame for this rests on Lysander, who persuaded them that "new times and new conditions called for new rules and a new policy."[2] Researches written from the point of view of such conceptions have very little affinity with science, and were written as sermons solely for the sake of the moral "lessons" that could be drawn from them. It was against such conceptions that the French historians of the period of the Restoration

[1] *Œuvres Complètes de l'abbé de Mably,* London, 1783 (Vol. iv), p. 3, 14–22, 24 *et* 192.
[2] *Ibid.,* p. 10.

revolted. After the stupendous events of the end of the eighteenth century it was absolutely impossible to think any longer that history was made by more or less prominent and more or less noble and enlightened individuals who at their own discretion imbued the unenlightened but obedient masses with certain sentiments and ideas. Moreover, this philosophy of history offended the plebeian pride of the bourgeois theoreticians. They were prompted by the same feelings that revealed themselves in the eighteenth century in the rise of bourgeois drama. In combating the old conceptions of history, Thierry used the same arguments that were advanced by Beaumarchais and others against the old æsthetics.[1] Lastly, the storms which France had just experienced very clearly revealed that the course of historical events was by no means determined solely by the conscious actions of men; this circumstance alone was enough to suggest the idea that these events were due to the influence of some hidden necessity, operating blindly, like the elemental forces of Nature, but in accordance with certain immutable laws. It is an extremely remarkable fact, which nobody, as far as we know, has pointed to before, that the French historians of the period of the Restoration applied the new conception of history as a process conforming to laws most consistently in their works on the French Revolution. This was the case, for example, in the works of Mignet. Chateaubriand called the new school of history *fatalistic*. Formulating the tasks

[1] Compare his first letter on *l'Histoire de France* with *l'Essai sur le genre dramatique sérieux* in the first volume of *Œuvres complètes de Beaumarchais*.

which it set the investigator, he said: "This system demands that the historian shall describe without indignation the most brutal atrocities, speak without love about the highest virtues and with his glacial eye see in social life only the manifestation of irresistible laws due to which every phenomenon occurs exactly as it inevitably had to occur."[1] This is wrong, of course. The new school did not demand that the historian should be impassive. Augustin Thierry even said quite openly that political passion, by sharpening the mind of the investigator, may serve as a powerful means of discovering the truth.[2] It is sufficient to make oneself only slightly familiar with the historical works of Guizot, Thierry or Mignet to see that they strongly sympathised with the bourgeoisie in its struggle against the lords temporal and spiritual, as well as with its efforts to suppress the demands of the rising proletariat. What is incontrovertible is the following: the new school of history arose in the twenties of the nineteenth century, i.e. when the bourgeoisie had already vanquished the aristocracy, although the latter was still striving to restore some of its old privileges. The proud consciousness of the victory of their class was reflected in all the arguments of the historians of the new school. And as the bourgeoisie was never distinguished for knightly chivalry, one can sometimes discern a note of harshness to the vanquished in the arguments of its

[1] *Œuvres complètes de Chateaubriand*, Paris, 1804, VII, p. 58. We also recommend the next page to the reader; one might think that it was written by Mr. N. Mikhailevsky.

[2] Cf. "Considérations sur l'histoire de France," appendix to *Récits des temps Mérévingiens*, Paris, 1840, p. 72.

scientific representatives. "*Le plus fort absorbe le plus faible,*" says Guizot, in one of his polemical pamphlets, "*et il est de droit*" (The strongest absorbs the weakest, and he has a right to do so). His attitude towards the working class is no less harsh. It was this harshness, which at times assumed the form of calm detachment, that misled Chateaubriand. Moreover, at that time it was not yet quite clear what was meant when it was said that history conformed to certain laws. Lastly, the new school may have appeared to be fatalistic because, striving firmly to adopt this point of view, it paid little attention to the great individuals in history.[1] Those who had been brought up on the historical ideas of the eighteenth century found it difficult to accept this. Objections to the views of the new historians poured in from all sides, and then the controversy flared up which, as we have seen, has not ended to this day.

In January, 1826, Sainte-Beuve, in a review, in the *Globe*, of the fifth and sixth volume of Mignet's *History of the French Revolution*, wrote as follows: "At any given moment a man may, by the sudden decision of his will, introduce into the course of events a new, unexpected and changeable force, which may alter that course,

[1] In a review of the third edition of Mignet's *History of the French Revolution*, Sainte-Beuve characterised that historian's attitude towards great men as follows: "In face of the vast and profound popular emotions which he had to describe, and of the impotence and nullity to which the sublimest genius and the saintliest virtue are reduced when the masses arise, he was seized with pity for men as individuals, could see in them, taken in isolation, only their weakness, and would not allow them to be capable of effective action, except through union with the multitude."

but which cannot be measured itself owing to its changeability." It must not be thought that Sainte-Beuve assumed that "sudden decisions" of human will occur without cause. No, that would have been too naïve. He merely asserted that the mental and moral qualities of a man who is playing a more or less important role in public life, his talent, knowledge, resoluteness or irresoluteness, courage or cowardice, etc., cannot help having a marked influence on the course and outcome of events; and yet these qualities cannot be explained solely by the general laws of development of a nation; they are always, and to a considerable degree, acquired as a result of the action of what may be called the accidents of private life. We will quote a few examples to explain this idea, which, incidentally, seems to me clear enough as it is.

During the War of the Austrian Succession the French Army achieved several brilliant victories and it seemed that France was in a position to compel Austria to cede fairly extensive territory in what is now Belgium; but Louis XV did not claim this territory because, as he said, he was fighting as a king and not as a merchant, and France got nothing out of the Peace of Aix-la-Chapelle. If, however, Louis XV had been a man of a different character, the territory of France would have been enlarged and as a result her economic and political development would have taken a somewhat different course.

As is well known, France waged the Seven Years' War in alliance with Austria. It is said that this alliance was concluded as a result of the strong pressure of Madame Pompadour, who had been extremely flattered by the

34

fact that, in a letter to her, proud Maria-Theresa had called her "cousin" or "dear friend" (*bien bonne amie*). Hence, one can say that had Louis XV been a man of stricter morals, or had he submitted less to his favourite's influence, Madame Pompadour would not have been able to influence the course of events to the extent that she did, and they would have taken a different turn.

Further, France was unsuccessful in the Seven Years' War: her generals suffered several very shameful defeats. Speaking generally, their conduct was very strange, to say the least. Richelieu engaged in plunder, and Soubise and Broglie were constantly hindering each other. For example, when Broglie was attacking the enemy at Villinghausen, Soubise heard the gunfire, but did not go to his comrade's assistance, as had been arranged, and as he undoubtedly should have done, and Broglie was obliged to retreat.[1] The extremely incompetent Soubise enjoyed the protection of the aforesaid Madame Pompadour. We can say again that had Louis XV been less lascivious, or had his favourite refrained from interfering in politics, events would not have turned out so unfavourably for France.

French historians say that there was no need at all for France to wage war on the European continent, and that she should have concentrated all her efforts on the sea in order to resist England's encroachments on her colonies. The fact that she acted differently was again due to the

[1] Incidentally, others say that Broglie was to blame for not waiting for his comrade, as he did not want to share the laurels of victory with him. This makes no difference to us, as it does not alter the case in the least.

inevitable Madame Pompadour, who wanted to please "her dear friend," Maria-Theresa. As a result of the Seven Years' War, France lost her best colonies, which undoubtedly greatly influenced the development of her economic relations. In this case, feminine vanity appears in the role of the influential "factor" of economic development.

Do we need any other examples? We will quote one more, perhaps the most astonishing one. During the aforesaid Seven Years' War, in August, 1761, the Austrian troops, having united with the Russian troops in Silesia, surrounded Frederick near Striegau. Frederick's position was desperate, but the Allies were tardy in attacking, and General Buturlin, after facing the enemy for twenty days, withdrew his troops from Silesia, leaving only a part of his forces as reinforcements for the Austrian General Laudon. Laudon captured Schweidnitz, near which Frederick was encamped, but this victory was of little importance. Suppose, however, Buturlin had been a man of firmer character? Suppose the Allies had attacked Frederick before he had time to entrench himself? They might have routed him, and he would have been compelled to yield to all the victors' demands. And this occurred barely a few months before a new accidental circumstance, the death of Empress Elizabeth, immediately changed the situation greatly in Frederick's favour. We would like to ask: What would have happened had Buturlin been a man of more resolute character, or had a man like Suvorov been in his place?

In examining the views of the "fatalist" historians, Sainte-Beuve gave expression to another opinion which is also worthy of attention. In the aforementioned review of Mignet's *History of the French Revolution*, he argued that the course and outcome of the French Revolution were determined, not only by the general causes which had given rise to the Revolution, and not only by the passions which in its turn the Revolution had roused, but also by numerous minor phenomena, which had escaped the attention of the investigator, and which were not even a part of social phenomena, properly so called. He wrote:

"While these passions" [roused by social phenomena] were operating, the physical and physiological forces of Nature were not inactive: stones continued to obey the law of gravity; the blood did not cease to circulate in the veins. Would not the course of events have changed had Mirabeau, say, not died of fever, had Robespierre been killed by the accidental fall of a brick or by a stroke of apoplexy, or if Bonaparte had been struck down by a bullet? And will you dare to assert that the outcome would have been the same? Given a sufficient number of accidents, similar to those I have assumed, the outcome might have been the very opposite of what, in your opinion, was inevitable. I have a right to assume the possibility of such accidents because they are precluded neither by the general causes of the Revolution nor by the passions roused by these general causes."

Then he goes on to quote the well-known observation that history would have taken an entirely different course had Cleopatra's nose been somewhat shorter; and, in conclusion, admitting that very much more could be

37

said in defence of Mignet's view, he again shows where this author goes wrong. Mignet ascribes solely to the action of general causes results which many other, minor, dark and elusive causes had helped to bring about; his stern logic, as it were, refuses to recognise the existence of anything that seems to him to be lacking in order and law.

VI

ARE Sainte-Beuve's objections sound? I think they contain a certain amount of truth. But what amount? To determine this we will first examine the idea that a man can "by the sudden decision of his will" introduce a new force into the course of events which is capable of changing their course considerably. We have quoted a number of examples, which, we think, very well explain this. Let us ponder over these examples.

Everybody knows that, during the reign of Louis XV, military affairs went steadily from bad to worse in France. As Henri Martin has observed, during the Seven Years' War, the French Army, which always had numerous prostitutes, tradesmen and servants in its train, and which had three times as many pack horses as saddle horses, had more resemblance to the hordes of Darius and Xerxes than to the armies of Turenne and Gustavus-Adolphus.[1] Archenholtz says in his history of this war

[1] *Histoire de France,* 4-ème edition, t. XV, pp. 520-1.

that the French officers, when appointed for guard duty, often deserted their posts to go dancing somewhere in the vicinity, and obeyed the orders of their superiors only when they thought fit. This deplorable state of military affairs was due to the deterioration of the aristocracy, which, however, continued to occupy all the high posts in the Army, and to the general dislocation of the "old order," which was rapidly drifting to its doom. These *general* causes alone would have been quite sufficient to make the outcome of the seven years war unfavourable to France. But undoubtedly the incompetence of generals like Soubise greatly increased the chances of failure for the French Army which these general causes already provided. Soubise retained his post, thanks to Madame Pompadour; and so we must count the proud Marquise as one of the "factors" significantly reinforcing the unfavourable influence of these general causes on the position of French affairs.

The Marquise de Pompadour was strong not by her own strength, but by the power of the king who was subject to her will. Can we say that the character of Louis XV was exactly what it was inevitably bound to be, in view of the general course of development of social relations in France? No, given the same course of development a King might have appeared in his place with a different attitude towards women. Sainte-Beuve would say that the action of obscure and intangible physiological causes was sufficient to account for this. And he would be right. But, if that is so, the conclusion emerges, that these obscure physiological causes, by affecting the progress and results of the Seven Years' War,

39

also in consequence affected the subsequent development of France, which would have proceeded differently if the Seven Years' War had not deprived her of a great part of her colonies. Does not this conclusion, we then ask, contradict the conception of a social development conforming to laws?

No, not in the least. The effect of personal peculiarities in the instances we have discussed, is undeniable; but no less undeniable is the fact that it could occur only *in the given social conditions*. After the battle of Rosbach the French became fiercely indignant with Soubise's position. Every day she received numbers of anonymous letters, full of threats and abuse. This very seriously disturbed Madame Pompadour; she began to suffer from insomnia.[1] Nevertheless, she continued to protect Soubise. In 1762, she remarked in one of her letters to him that he was not justifying the hopes that had been placed in him, but she added: "Have no fear, however, I will take care of your interests and try to reconcile you with the King."[2] As you see, she did not yield to public opinion. Why did she not yield? Probably because French society of that day *had nò means of compelling* her to do so. But why was French society of that day unable to do so? It was prevented from doing so by its form of organisation, which in turn, was determined by the relation of social forces in France at that time. Hence, it is the relation of social forces which, in the last analysis, explains the fact that Louis XV's character, and the caprices of his favourite, could have such a deplorable influence on the

[1] Cf. *Mémoires de madame du Haliffet*, Paris, 1824, p. 181.
[2] Cf. *Lettres de la marquise de Pompadour*, London, 1772, t. I.

fate of France. Had it not been the King who had a weakness for the fair sex, but the King's cook or groom, it would not have had any historical significance. Clearly, it is not the weakness that is important here, but the social position of the person afflicted with it. The reader will understand that these arguments can be applied to all the above-quoted examples. In these arguments it is necessary to change only what needs changing, for example, to put Russia in the place of France, Buturlin in place of Soubise, etc. That is why we will not repeat them.

It follows, then, that by virtue of particular traits of their character, individuals can influence the fate of society. Sometimes this influence is very considerable; but the possibility of exercising this influence, and its extent, are determined by the form of organisation of society, by the relation of forces within it. The character of an individual is a "factor" in social development only where, when, and to the extent that social relations permit it to be such.

We may be told that the extent of personal influence may also be determined by the talents of the individual. We agree. But the individual can display his talents only when he occupies the position in society necessary for this. Why was the fate of France in the hands of a man who totally lacked the ability and desire to serve society? Because such was the form of organisation of that society. It is the form of organisation that in any given period determines the role and, consequently, the social significance that may fall to the lot of talented or incompetent individuals.

But if the role of individuals is determined by

the form of organisation of society, how can their social influence, which is determined by the role they play, contradict the conception of social development as a process expressing laws? It does not contradict it; on the contrary, it serves as one of its most vivid illustrations.

But here we must observe the following. The possibility—determined by the form of organisation of society —that individuals may exercise social influence, opens the door to the influence of so-called *accident* upon the historical destiny of nations. Louis XV's lasciviousness was an inevitable consequence of the state of his physical constitution, but in relation to the general course of France's development the state of his constitution was *accidental*. Nevertheless, as we have said, it did influence the fate of France and served as one of the causes which determined this fate. The death of Mirabeau, of course, was due to pathological processes which obeyed definite laws. The inevitability of these processes, however, did not arise out of the general course of France's development, but out of certain particular features of the celebrated orator's constitution, and out of the physical conditions under which he had contracted his disease. In relation to the general course of France's development these features and conditions were *accidental*. And yet, Mirabeau's death influenced the further course of the revolution and served as one of the causes which determined it.

Still more astonishing was the effect of accidental causes in the above-mentioned example of Frederick II, who succeeded in extricating himself from an extremely difficult situation only because of Buturlin's irresolution. Even in relation to the general cause of Russia's development Buturlin's appointment may have been accidental, in the sense that we have defined that term, and, of course, it had no relation whatever to the general course of Prussia's development. Yet it is not improbable that Buturlin's irresolution saved Frederick from a desperate situation. Had Suvorov been in Buturlin's place, the history of Prussia might have taken a different course. It follows, then, that sometimes the fate of nations depends on accidents, which may be called *accidents of the second degree*. "*In allem Endlichen ist ein Element des Zufälligen*," said Hegel (In everything finite there are accidental elements). In science we deal only with the "finite"; hence we can say that all the processes studied by science contain some accidental elements. Does not this preclude the scientific cognition of phenomena? No. *Accident is something relative.* It appears only at the point of intersection of *inevitable* processes. For the inhabitants of Mexico and Peru, the appearance of Europeans in America was *accidental* in the sense that it did not follow from the social development of these countries. But the passion for navigation which possessed West Europeans at the end of the Middle Ages was not accidental; nor was the fact that the European forces easily overcame the resistance of the natives. The consequences of the conquest of Mexico and Peru by Europeans were also not accidental; in the last analysis, these consequences were determined by the resultant of two forces: the economic position of the conquered countries on the one hand, and the economic position of the conquerors on

43

the other. And these forces, like their resultant, can fully serve as objects of scientific investigation.

The accidents of the Seven Years' War exercised considerable influence upon the subsequent history of Prussia. But their influence would have been entirely different at a different stage of Prussia's development. Here, too, the accidental consequences were determined by the resultant of two forces: the social-political conditions of Prussia on the one hand, and the social-political condition of the European countries that influenced her, on the other. Hence, here, too, accidents do not in the least hinder the scientific investigation of phenomena.

We know now that individuals often exercise considerable influence upon the fate of society, but this influence is determined by the internal structure of that society and by its relation to other societies. But this is not all that has to be said about the role of the individual in history. We must approach this question from still another side.

Sainte-Beuve thought that had there been a sufficient number of petty and dark causes of the kind that he had mentioned, the outcome of the French Revolution would have been the *opposite* of what we know it to have been. This is a great mistake. No matter how intricately the petty, psychological and physiological causes may have been interwoven, they would not under any circumstances have eliminated the great social needs that gave rise to the French Revolution; and as long as these needs remained unsatisfied the revolutionary movement in France would have continued. To make the outcome of this movement the opposite of what it was, the

44

needs that gave rise to it would have had to be the opposite of what they were; and this, of course, no combination of petty causes would ever be able to bring about.

The causes of the French Revolution lay in the character of the *social relations*; and the petty causes assumed by Sainte-Beuve could lie only in the *personal qualities of individuals*. The final cause of social relationships lies in the state of the productive forces. This depends on the qualities of individuals only in the sense, perhaps, that these individuals possess more or less talent for making technical improvements, discoveries and inventions. Sainte-Beuve did not have these qualities in mind. No other qualities, however, enable individuals directly to influence the state of productive forces, and hence, the social relations which they determine, i.e. *economic relations*. No matter what the qualities of the given individual may be, they cannot eliminate the given economic relations if the latter conform to the given state of productive forces. But the personal qualities of individuals make them more or less fit to satisfy those social needs which arise out of the given economic relations, or to counteract such satisfaction. The urgent social need of France at the end of the eighteenth century was the substitution for the obsolete political institutions of new institutions that would conform more to her economic system. The most prominent and useful public men of that time were those who were more capable than others of helping to satisfy this most urgent need. We will assume that Mirabeau, Robespierre and Napoleon were men of that type. What would have happened had premature death not removed

45

Mirabeau from the political stage? The constitutional monarchist party would have retained its considerable power for a longer period; its resistance to the republicans would, therefore, have been more energetic. But that is all. No Mirabeau could, at that time, have averted the triumph of the republicans. Mirabeau's power rested entirely on the sympathy and confidence of the people; but the people wanted a republic, as the Court irritated them by its obstinate defence of the old order. As soon as the people had become convinced that Mirabeau did not sympathise with their republican strivings they would have ceased to sympathise with him; and then the great orator would have lost nearly all influence, and in all probability would have fallen a victim to the very movement that he would vainly have tried to check. Approximately the same thing may be said about Robespierre. Let us assume that he was an absolutely indispensable force in his party; but even so, he was not the only force. If the accidental fall of a brick had killed him, say, in January, 1793, his place would, of course, have been taken by somebody else, and although this person might have been inferior to him in every respect, nevertheless, events would have taken *the same course* as they did when Robespierre was alive. For example, even under these circumstances the Gironde would probably not have escaped defeat; but it is possible that Robespierre's party would have lost power somewhat earlier and we would now be speaking, not of the Thermidor reaction, but of the Floreal, Prairial or Messidor reaction. Perhaps some will say that with his inexorable Terror, Robespierre did not delay but

46

hastened the downfall of his party. We will not stop to examine this supposition here; we will accept it as if it were quite sound. In that case we must assume that Robespierre's party would have fallen not in Thermidor, but in Fructidor, Vendémiaine or Brumaire. In short, it may have fallen sooner or perhaps later, but it certainly would have fallen, because the section of the people which supported Robespierre's party was totally unprepared to hold power for a prolonged period. At all events, results "opposite" to those which arose from Robespierre's energetic action are out of the question.

Nor could they have arisen even if Bonaparte had been struck down by a bullet, let us say, at the Battle of Arcole. What he did in the Italian and other campaigns other generals would have done. Probably they would not have displayed the same talent as he did, and would not have achieved such brilliant victories; nevertheless the French Republic would have emerged victorious from the wars it waged at that time, because its soldiers were incomparably the best in Europe. As for the 18th of Brumaire and its influence on the internal life of France, here, too, *in essence*, the general course and outcome of events would probably have been the same as they were under Napoleon. The Republic, mortally wounded by the events of the 9th of Thermidor, was slowly dying. The Directoire was unable to restore order which the bourgeoisie, having rid itself of the rule of the aristocracy, now desired most of all. To restore order a *"good sword,"* as Siéyès expressed it, was needed. At first it was thought that general Jourdan would serve in this virtuous role, but when he was killed at Novi, the names of Moreau,

47

MacDonald and Bernadotte were mentioned.[1] Bonaparte was only mentioned later: and had he been killed, like Jourdan, he would not have been mentioned at all, and some other "sword" would have been put forward. It goes without saying that the man whom events had elevated to the position of dictator must have been tirelessly aspiring to power himself, energetically pushing aside and ruthlessly crushing all who stood in his way. Bonaparte was a man of iron energy and was remorseless in the pursuit of his goal. But there were not a few energetic, talented and ambitious egoists in those days besides him. The place Bonaparte succeeded in occupying would, probably, not have remained vacant. Let us assume that the other general who had secured this place would have been more peaceful than Napoleon, that he would not have roused the whole of Europe against himself, and therefore, would have died in the Tuileries and not on the island of St. Helena. In that case, the Bourbons would not have returned to France at all; for them, such a result would certainly have been the "opposite" of what it was. In its relation to the internal life of France as a whole, however, this result would have differed little from the actual result. After the "good sword" had restored order and had consolidated the power of the bourgeoisie, the latter would have tired soon of its barrack-room habits and despotism. A liberal movement would have arisen, similar to the one that arose after the Restoration; the fight would have gradually flared up, and as "good swords" are not

[1] La vie en France sous le premier Empire by de Broc, Paris, 1895, pp. 35–6 et seq.

distinguished for their yielding nature, the virtuous Louis-Philippe would, perhaps, have ascended the throne of his dearly beloved kinsmen, not in 1830, but in 1820, or in 1825. All such changes in the course of events might, to some extent, have influenced the subsequent political, and through it, the economic life of Europe. Nevertheless, under no circumstances would the final outcome of the revolutionary movement have been the "opposite" of what it was. Owing to the specific qualities of their minds and characters, influential individuals can change the *individual features of events and some of their particular consequences,* but they cannot change their general *trend,* which is determined by other forces.

VII

FURTHERMORE, we must also note the following. In discussing the role great men play in history, we nearly always fall victims to a sort of optical illusion, to which it will be useful to draw the reader's attention.

In coming out in the role of the "good sword" to save public order, Napoleon prevented all the other generals from playing this role, and some of them might have performed it in the same way, or almost the same way, as he did. Once the public need for an energetic military ruler was satisfied, the social organisation barred the road to the position of military ruler for all other talented soldiers. Its power became a power that was unfavourable to the appearance of other talents of a similar kind. This is the cause of the optical illusion, which we have mentioned. Napoleon's personal power presents itself to us in an extremely magnified form, for we place to his account the social power which had brought him to the front and supported him. Napoleon's power appears to us to be something quite exceptional because the other powers similar to it did not pass from the potential to the real. And when we are asked, "What would have happened if there had been no Napoleon?" our *imagination* becomes confused and it seems to us that without him the social movement upon which his power and influence were based could not have taken place.

In the history of the development of human intellect, the success of some individual hinders the success of another individual very much more rarely. But even here we are not free from the above-mentioned optical illusion. When a given state of society sets certain problems before its intellectual representatives, the attention of prominent minds is concentrated upon them until these problems are solved. As soon as they have succeeded in solving them, their attention is transferred to another object. By solving a problem a given talent A diverts the attention of talent B from the problem already solved to another problem. And when we are asked: What would have happened if A had died before he had solved problem X?—we imagine that the thread of development of the human intellect would have been broken. We forget that had A died B, or C, or D might have tackled the problem, and the thread of intellectual development would have remained intact in spite of A's premature demise.

In order that a man who possesses a particular kind of talent may, by means of it, greatly influence the course of events, two conditions are needed. First, this talent must make him more conformable to the social needs of the given epoch than anyone else: if Napoleon had possessed the musical gifts of Beethoven instead of his own military genius he would not, of course, have become an emperor. Second, the existing social order must not bar the road to the person possessing the talent which is needed and useful precisely at the given time. This very *Napoleon* would have died as the barely known General, or Colonel, *Bonaparte* had the old order in France existed another seventy-five years.[1] In 1789, Davout, Désaix, Marmont and MacDonald were subalterns; Bernadotte was a *sergeant-major*; Hoche, Marceau, Lefebre, Pichegru, Ney, Masséna, Murat and Soult were *non-commissioned officers*; Augereau was a *fencing master*; Lannes was a *dyer*; Gouvion Saint-Cyr was an *actor*; Jourdan was a *peddler*; Bessières was a *barber*; Brune was a *compositor*; Joubert and Junot were *law students*; Kléber was an *architect*; Martier did not see any military service until the revolution.[2]

Had the old order continued to exist up to our days it would never have occurred to any of us that in France, at the end of the last century, certain actors, compositors,

[1] Probably Napoleon would have gone to Russia, *where he had intended to go just a few years before the Revolution.* Here, no doubt, he would have distinguished himself in action against the Turks or the Caucasian highlanders, but nobody here would have thought that this poor, but capable, officer could, under favourable circumstances, have become the ruler of the world.

[2] Cf. *Histoire de France*, V. Duruy, Paris, 1893, t. II, pp. 524-5.

barbers, dyers, lawyers, peddlers and fencing masters had been potential military geniuses.[1]

Stendhal observed that a man who was born at the same time as Titian, i.e. in 1477, could have lived forty years with Raphael, who died in 1520, and with Leonardo da Vinci, who died in 1519; that he could have spent many years with Corregio, who died in 1534, and with Michelangelo, who lived until 1563; that he would have been no more than thirty-four years of age when Giorgione died; that he could have been acquainted with Tintoretto, Bassano, Veronese, Julian Romano and Andrea del Sarto; that, in short, he would have been the contemporary of all the great painters, with the exception of those who belonged to the Bologna School, which arose a full century later.[2] Similarly, it may be said that a man who was born in the same year as Wouwermann could have been personally acquainted with nearly all the great Dutch painters;[3] and a man of the same age as

[1] In the reign of Louis XV, only one representative of the third estate, Chevert, could rise to the rank of lieutenant-general. In the reign of Louis XVI it was even more difficult for members of this estate to make a military career. Cf. Rambeaud, *Histoire de la civilisation française*, 6th edition, t. II, p. 226.

[2] *Histoire de la Peinture en Italie*, Paris, 1889, pp. 23–5.

[3] Terburg, Brower and Rembrandt were born in 1608; Adrian Van-Ostade and Ferdinand Bol were born in 1610; Van der Hölst and Gerard Dow were born in 1615; Wouwermann was born in 1620; Werniks, Everdingen and Painaker were born in 1621; Bergham was born in 1624 and Paul Potter in 1629; Jan Steen was born in 1626; Ruisdal and Metsu were born in 1630; Van der Haiden was born in 1637; Hobbema was born in 1638 and Adrian Van der Velde was born in 1639.

Shakespeare would have been the contemporary of a number of remarkable playwrights.[1]

It has long been observed that great talents appear everywhere, whenever the social conditions favourable to their development exist. This means that every man of talent who *actually appears*, i.e. every man of talent who becomes a *social force*, is the product of *social relations*. Since this is the case, it is clear why talented people can, as we have said, change only individual features of events, but not their general trend; *they are themselves the product of this trend; were it not for that trend they would never have crossed the threshold that divides the potential from the real.*

It goes without saying that there is talent and talent. "When a fresh step in the development of civilisation calls into being a new form of art," rightly says Taine, "scores of talents who only half express social thought appear around one or two geniuses who express it perfectly."[2] If, owing to certain mechanical or physiological causes unconnected with the general course of the social-political and intellectual development of Italy, Raphael, Michelangelo and Leonardo da Vinci had died in their infancy, Italian art would have been less perfect, but the general trend of its development in the period of the Renaissance would have remained the same. Raphael,

[1] "Shakespeare, Beaumont, Fletcher, Jonson, Webster, Massinger, Ford, Middleton and Heywood, who appeared at the same time, or following each other, represented the new generation which, owing to its favourable position, flourished on the soil which had been prepared by the efforts of the preceding generation." Taine, *Histoire de la littérature anglaise*, Paris, 1863, t. I, p. 468.

[2] Taine, "*Histoire de la littérature anglaise*," Paris, 1863, t. I, p. 5.

Leonardo da Vinci and Michelangelo did not create this trend; they were merely its best representatives. True, usually a whole school springs up around a man of genius, and his pupils try to copy his methods to the minutest details; that is why the gap that would have been left in Italian art in the period of the Renaissance by the early death of Raphael, Michelangelo and Leonardo da Vinci would have strongly influenced many of the secondary features of its subsequent history. But in essence, there would have been no change in this history, provided there were no important change in the general course of the intellectual development of Italy due to general causes.

It is well known, however, that quantitative differences ultimately pass into qualitative differences. This is true everywhere, and is therefore true in history. A given trend in art may remain without any remarkable expression if an unfavourable combination of circumstances carries away, one after the other, several talented people who might have given it expression. But the premature death of such talented people can prevent the artistic expression of this trend only if it is too shallow to produce new talent. As, however, the depth of any given trend in literature and art is determined by its importance for the class, or stratum, whose tastes it expresses, and by the social role played by that class or stratum, here, too, in the last analysis, everything depends upon the course of social development and on the relation of social forces.

VIII

THUS, the personal qualities of leading people determine the individual features of historical events; and the accidental element, in the sense that we have indicated, always plays some role in the course of these events, the trend of which is determined in the last analysis by so-called general causes, i.e. actually by the development of productive forces and the mutual relations between men in the social-economic process of production. Casual phenomena and the personal qualities of celebrated people are ever so much more noticeable than deep-lying general causes. The eighteenth century pondered but little over these general causes, and claimed that history was explained by the conscious actions and "passions" of historical personages. The philosophers of that century asserted that history might have taken an entirely different course as a result of the most insignificant causes; for example, if some "atom" had started playing pranks in some ruler's head (an idea expressed more than once in *Système de la Nature*).

The adherents of the new trend in the science of history began to argue that history could not have taken any other course than the one it has taken, notwithstanding all "atoms." Striving to emphasise the effect of general causes as much as possible, they ignored the personal qualities of historical personages. According to their argument, historical events would not have been affected in the least by the substitution of some persons for others, more or less capable.[1] But if we make such an assumption then we must admit that the *personal element is of no significance whatever in history*, and that everything can be reduced to the operation of general causes, to the general laws of historical progress. This would be going to an extreme which leaves no room for the particle of truth contained in the opposite opinion. It is precisely for this reason that the opposite opinion retained some right to existence. The collision between these two opinions assumed the form of an antinomy, the first part of which was general laws, and the second part was the activities of individuals. From the point of view of the second part of the antinomy, history was simply a chain of accidents; from the point of view of the first part it seemed that even the individual features of historical events were determined by the operation of general causes. But if the individual features of events are determined by the influence of general causes and do not depend upon the personal qualities of historical personages, it follows that these features are *determined by general causes* and cannot be changed, no matter how much these personages may change. Thus, the theory assumes a *fatalistic* character.

This did not escape the attention of its opponents. Sainte-Beuve compared Mignet's conception of history

[1] According to their argument, i.e. when they began to discuss the tendency of historical events to conform to laws. When, however, some of them simply described these phenomena, they sometimes ascribed even exaggerated significance to the personal element. What interests us now, however, are not their descriptions, but their arguments.

with that of Bossuet. Bossuet thought that the force which causes historical events to take place comes from above, that events serve to express the divine will. Mignet sought for this force in the human passions, which are displayed in historical events as inexorably and immutably as the forces of Nature. But both regarded history as a chain of phenomena which could not have been different, no matter under what circumstances; both were fatalists; in this respect, the philosopher was not far removed from the priest (*le philosophe se rapproche du prêtre*).

This reproach was justified as long as the doctrine, that social phenomena conformed to certain laws, reduced the influence of the personal qualities of prominent historical individuals to a cipher. And the impression made by this reproach was all the more strong for the reason that the historians of the new school, like the historians and philosophers of the eighteenth century, regarded *human nature* as a higher instance, from which all the *general causes* of historical movement sprang, and to which they were subordinated. As the French Revolution had shown that historical events are not determined by the *conscious* actions of men alone, Mignet and Guizot, and the other historians of the same trend, put in the forefront the effect of the *passions*, which often rebelled against all control of the mind. But if tne passions are the final and most general cause of historical events, then why is Sainte-Beuve wrong in asserting that the outcome of the French Revolution might have been the opposite of what we know it was if there had been individuals capable of imbuing the French people with

57

passions opposite to those which had excited them? Mignet would have said: Because other passions could not have excited the French people at that time owing to the very qualities of human nature. In a certain sense this would have been true. But this truth would have had a strongly fatalistic tinge, for it would have been on a par with the thesis that the history of mankind, in all its details, is predetermined by the *general* qualities of human nature. Fatalism would have appeared here as the result of the disappearance of the *individual in the general.* Incidentally, it is always the result of such a disappearance. It is said: "If all social phenomena are inevitable, then our activities cannot have any significance." This is a correct idea wrongly formulated. We ought to say: if everything occurs as a result of the *general,* then the *individual,* including my efforts, is of no significance. *This* deduction is correct; but it is incorrectly employed. It is senseless when applied to the modern materialist conception of history, in which there is room also for the *individual.* But it was justified when applied to the views of the French historians in the period of the Restoration.

At the present time, human nature can no longer be regarded as the final and most general cause of historical progress: if it is constant, then it cannot explain the extremely changeable course of history; if it is changeable, then obviously its changes are themselves determined by historical progress. At the present time we must regard the development of productive forces as the final and most general cause of the historical progress of mankind, and it is these productive forces that determine the consecutive changes in the social relations of men. Parallel with this *general* cause there are *particular* causes, i.e. *the historical situation* in which the development of the productive forces of a given nation proceeds and which, in the last analysis, is itself created by the development of these forces among other nations, i.e. the same general cause.

Finally, the influence of the *particular* causes is supplemented by the operation of *individual* causes, i.e. the personal qualities of public men and other "accidents," thanks to which events finally assume their *individual features*. Individual causes cannot bring about fundamental changes in the operation of *general and particular* causes which, moreover, determine the trend and limits of the influence of individual causes. Nevertheless, there is no doubt that history would have had different features had the individual causes which had influenced it been replaced by other causes of the same order.

Monod and Lamprecht still adhere to the human nature point of view. Lamprecht has categorically, and more than once, declared that in his opinion social mentality is the fundamental cause of historical phenomena. This is a great mistake, and as a result of this mistake the desire, very laudable in itself, to take into account the sum total of social life may lead only to vapid eclecticism or, among the most consistent, to Kablitz's arguments concerning the relative significance of the mind and the senses.

But let us return to our subject. A great man is great not because his personal qualities give individual features to great historical events, but because he possesses qualities which make him most capable of serving the great social needs of his time, needs which arose as a result of general and particular causes. Carlyle, in his well-known book on heroes and hero-worship, calls great men *beginners*. This is a very apt description. A great man is precisely a beginner because he sees *further* than others, and desires things *more strongly* than others. He solves the scientific problems brought up by the preceding process of intellectual development of society; he points to the new social needs created by the preceding development of social relationships; he takes the initiative in satisfying these needs. He is a hero. But he is not a hero in the sense that he can stop, or change, the natural course of things, but in the sense that his activities are the conscious and free expression of this inevitable and unconscious course. Herein lies all his significance; herein lies his whole power. But this significance is colossal, and the power is terrible.

Bismarck said that we cannot make history and must wait while it is being made. But who makes history? It is made by the *social man*, who is its *sole "factor."* The social man creates his own, i.e. social, relationships. But if in a given period he creates given relationships and not others, there must be some cause for it, of course; it is determined by the state of his productive forces. No great man can foist on society relations which *no longer* conform to the state of these forces, or which *do not yet* conform to them. In this sense, indeed, he cannot make history, and in this sense he would advance the hands of his clock in vain; he would not hasten the passage of time, nor turn it back. Here Lamprecht is quite right:

even at the height of his power Bismarck could not cause Germany to revert to natural economy.

Social relationships have their inherent logic: as long as people live in given mutual relationships they will feel, think and act in a given way, and no other. Attempts on the part of public men to combat this logic would also be fruitless; the natural course of things (i.e. this logic of social relationships) would reduce all his efforts to naught. But if I know in what direction social relations are changing owing to given changes in the social-economic process of production, I also know in what direction social mentality is changing; consequently, I am able to influence it. Influencing social mentality means influencing historical events. Hence, in a certain sense, I *can make history*, and there is no need for me to wait while "it is being made."

Monod believes that really important events and individuals in history are important only as signs and symbols of the development of institutions and economic conditions. This is a correct although very inexactly expressed idea; but precisely because this idea is correct it is wrong to oppose the activities of great men to "the *slow progress*" of the conditions and institutions mentioned. The more or less slow changes in "economic conditions" periodically confront society with the necessity of more or less rapidly changing its institutions. This change never takes place "by itself"; it always needs the intervention of *men*, who are thus confronted with great social problems. And it is those men who do more than others to facilitate the solution of these problems who are called great men. But *solving a problem* does not mean being only a "symbol" and a "sign" of the fact that it has been solved.

We think that Monod opposed the one to the other mainly because he was carried away by the pleasant catchword, "*slow*." Many modern evolutionists are very fond of this catchword. *Psychologically*, this passion is comprehensible: it *inevitably* arises in the respectable milieu of moderation and punctiliousness. . . . But *logically* it does not bear examination, as Hegel proved.

And it is not only for "beginners," not only for "great" men that a broad field of activity is open. It is open for all those who have eyes to see, ears to hear and hearts to love their neighbours. The concept *great* is a relative concept. In the ethical sense every man is great who, to use the Biblical phrase, "lays down his life for his friend."

CPSIA information can be obtained
at www.ICGtesting.com
Printed in the USA
BVOW08s2327071117
499803BV00001B/69/P